What Are Germs?

Dr. Alvin Silverstein,

Virginia Silverstein, and

Laura Silverstein Nunn

My Health
Franklin Watts

A Division of Scholastic Inc.

New York • Toronto • London • Auckland • Sydney

Mexico City • New Delhi • Hong Kong

Danbury, Connecticut

Photographs © 2002: Corbis Images: 32; Custom Medical Stock Photo/ T.J. O'Donnell: 34; Peter Arnold Inc.: 21 (Matt Meadows), 7 (David Scharf), 26 (Volker Steger); Photo Researchers, NY: 17, 28 (Biophoto Associates), 4 (Ken Lax), 10 top (Microfield Scientific LTD/SPL), 31 (Dr. Gopal Murty/SPL); PhotoEdit: 8 (Spencer Grant), 29, 35 (Michael Newman); Stock Boston: 15 (Mark C. Burnett), 12, 40 (Bob Daemmrich), 37 (Aaron Haupt); Superstock, Inc.: 11, 13, 20, 25; Visuals Unlimited: 14 (Fred Hossler), 6, 18 (K.G. Murti), 24 (Larry Stepanowicz), 22 (D. Yeske).

Cartoons by Rick Stromoski

Library of Congress Cataloging-in Publication Data

Silverstein, Alvin.
    What Are Germs? / by Dr. Alvin Silverstein, Virginia Silverstein and Laura Silverstein Nunn.
        p. (cm). – (My Health)
    Includes bibliographical references and index.
Summary: Explains the science of germs and emphasizes the importance of maintaining personal health.
    ISBN 0-531-12047-3 (lib. bdg.)   0-531-16640-6 (pbk.)
    1. Microorganisms—Juvenile literature. 2. Communicable diseases—Juvenile literature. [1. Microorganisms. 2. Communicable Diseases. 3. Diseases] I. Silverstein, Virginia B. II. Nunn, Laura Silverstein. III. Title. IV. Series.
    QR57 .S538 2002
    616'.01—dc21   2001005364

C●ntents

Germs Make You Sick

You wake up one morning and can hardly get out of bed. Your throat feels scratchy, and your nose is all stuffed up. You get a tissue to blow your nose, and...achoo! You're just in time to catch an unexpected sneeze. You don't feel like yourself at all today—you're sick.

Everybody knows that germs can make you sick. Germs are **microorganisms**—tiny creatures that cannot be seen without a microscope. They are everywhere—in the air you breathe, in the food you eat, in the water you drink, and on everything you touch.

MICRO-ORGANISM TALLY

◀ **A stuffed-up nose is just one symptom of a cold.**

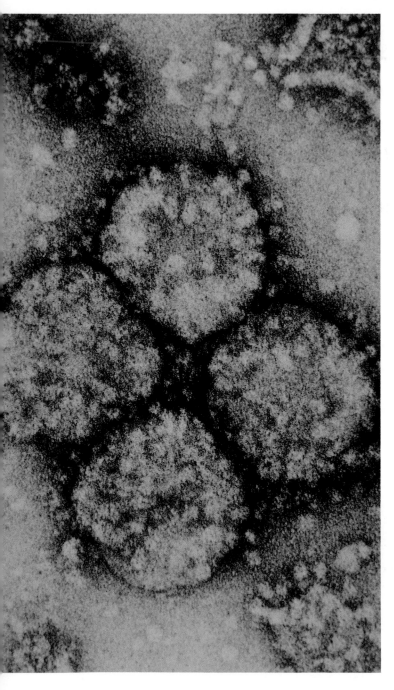

Even though germs are all around you, they don't always make you sick. Most of the time, your body does a good job keeping out harmful germs. But sometimes germs do get in and can make you feel sick. Fortunately, your body has built-in defenses against germs that fight very hard so you can feel well again.

Sometimes germs make you so sick that you need to see a doctor. You may have to take medication to kill the germs.

There are many things you can do to protect yourself against germs. Some of these things can help you get better faster, and others help you avoid getting sick in the first place.

This virus causes a common cold and can be easily spread from person to person.

All About Germs

Under the right conditions—warmth, moisture, and plenty of food—microorganisms can multiply and thrive. Although some microorganisms can live on their own in the environment, many of them can live only inside a *host*—a living animal or plant.

Germ Hideouts

Light can kill many germs. Most germs grow best in warm, dark, moist places, such as your nose, mouth, or armpits. In your home, microorganisms may live and multiply in cupboards, closets, or under the bed. Lots of germs can grow on the sponge you use to wipe the kitchen sink and counters. The sponge is damp and contains bits of food that germs can feed on. When a sponge or dishcloth gets smelly, throw it out or wash it thoroughly with a **disinfectant** solution that kills bacteria and fungi.

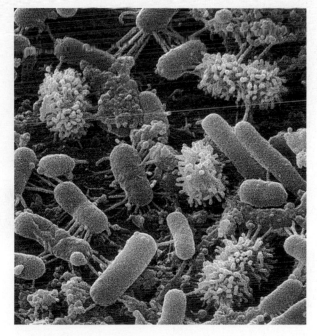

These bacteria are growing on a kitchen sponge.

7

Germs are such tiny creatures that they can enter into your body without your even noticing them. You may breathe in microorganisms floating in the air or swallow them with food or water. They may get in if you touch something covered with germs, and then rub your nose, mouth, or eyes with your fingers. A cut or scrape may also make it easy for germs to enter your body. Even a mosquito can inject germs into your skin when it bites you.

Germs can enter your body when you touch your eyes, nose, or mouth.

Activity 1:
How Well Do You Wash Your Hands?

Studies have shown that many people do not wash their hands after going to the bathroom. Handwashing is a great way to prevent the spread of germs found in body wastes. But even people who do wash their hands may not do it well enough to get rid of the germs.

For this activity, you will need a tube of washable paint, a sink, soap, a watch with a second hand, and a friend. Put a dab of paint in one palm and smear it all over both of your hands, including the backs and the fingers. Now wash your hands with soap the way you normally do, and have a friend time how long it takes. Look at your hands. Did you wash off all of the paint? Probably not. Most people spend less than 30 seconds on handwashing. That is not enough time to get rid of all the germs. Now wash your hands some more and have your friend time how long it takes until all the paint is gone. Add that to the time you spent on the first handwashing. The total is how long you need to spend washing your hands to get them clean and germ-free.

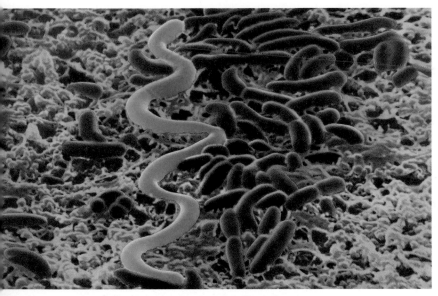
This bacterium is spiral shaped.

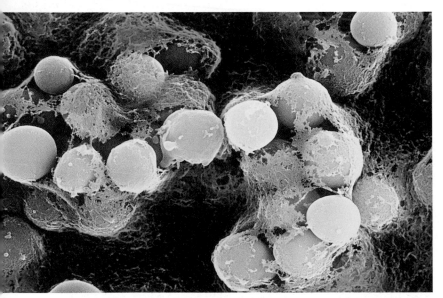
These round bacteria cause strep throat infections.

When germs get inside your body, they can cause some real trouble. They can thrive inside your body because it is warm, moist, and full of food. The nourishment they get from you gives them the energy they need to survive and reproduce.

The two kinds of germs that most often cause harm are **bacteria** and **viruses**. Under a microscope, not all bacteria look the same. Some look like little short, straight sticks or rods. Others are shaped like little round balls. Still others are spiral shaped and look like little corkscrews. Some bacteria look like bent rods or commas.

If you look closely through a microscope, you will see that bacteria are single-celled creatures. Amazingly, just a single cell can do everything it needs to survive on its own. A bacterium can find shelter, get food, grow, and reproduce.

When bacteria get inside your body, they can multiply quickly. Each bacterium reproduces by dividing into two smaller bacteria. Each one grows quickly until it is ready to divide too. Some bacteria give off poisons, called **toxins**, which can damage or kill body cells. When enough cells are harmed, you feel sick.

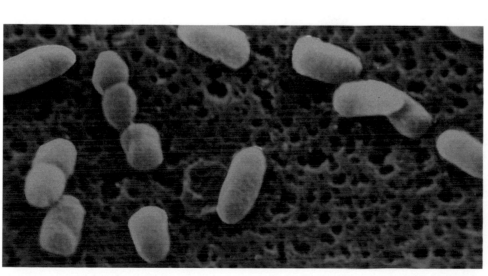

These bacteria are shaped like little rods.

Helpful Bacteria

Not all bacteria are bad. In fact, most do not harm us at all. Some of them are even helpful. Certain bacteria in your intestines help to destroy other microorganisms that could be harmful to you. Others help to break down food to make it easier to digest. Still others make important vitamins, such as B vitamins and vitamin K, that make us healthy and strong.

Some bacteria help to clean up the environment. **Decay bacteria** break down animal wastes and the bodies of dead plants and animals. Without them, the earth would be covered with wastes and dead plants and animals. Decay bacteria are also excellent recyclers, returning materials to the water or soil so that they can be used again by new plants and animals.

Other bacteria that live in the soil, the nitrogen-fixing bacteria, help plants by taking nitrogen gas from the atmosphere and turning it into a form that plants can use.

Decay bacteria break down plant matter.

Viruses are much tinier than bacteria. Bacteria can be seen under an ordinary microscope, but you need to use a much more powerful microscope to look at viruses. Under a strong microscope, some viruses look like balls with spikes sticking out all over. Others look like loaves of bread, coiled springs, or even tadpoles.

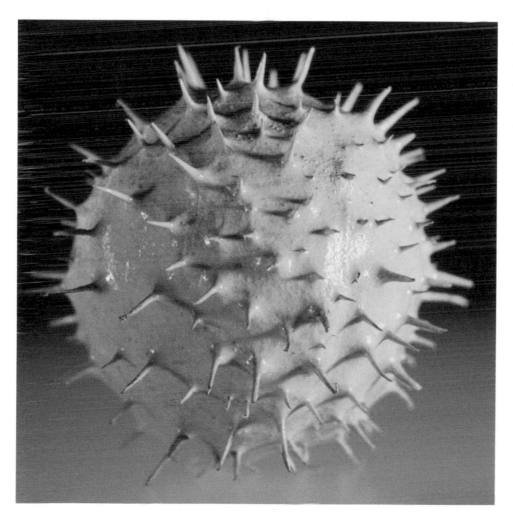

The AIDS virus is one type of virus that looks like a ball with spikes.

Just Add Water

Many living things would die without water. But many fungi can survive dry periods by changing into a resting stage. They seem dead, but as soon as they have water again, they start to grow actively.

INSTANT FUNGI JUST ADD WATER

Although refrigerating food may keep bacteria from growing, it won't keep mold from growing on fruits and vegetables or in a jar of jelly. Some fungi have even been found growing around the hot springs of volcanoes.

Amoebas are tiny, one-celled creatures, shaped like a blob of jelly. Most live in ponds, lakes, or oceans. But some amoebas are disease-producing germs that cause trouble when they get into peoples' bodies. Amoebas belong to a group of animal-like microorganisms called **protozoa**. Other kinds of protozoa can cause serious diseases, such as sleeping sickness and malaria.

Your Body's Defenses

When bacteria and viruses get inside you, your body fights back. Some of the germs that enter your nose get trapped in bristly hairs inside your nostrils. Germs that make it past these hairs fall into a gooey fluid that covers the lining of your nose. This fluid is called **mucus**. Mucus carries the trapped germs to the back of your throat. When you swallow, these germs—plus germs that have entered your mouth—travel to your stomach where they are destroyed in a pool of acid.

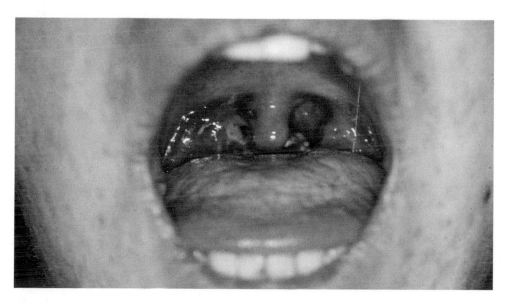

Mucus carries germs to the back of your throat.

Other invading germs are destroyed by your **immune system**. When viruses and bacteria get inside your body cells, those cells send out chemicals to alert nearby cells about the foreign invaders. Some of these chemicals make fluid leak out of the blood vessels into the body tissues, making them swollen. The tissues also get hot and red. This process is called **inflammation**. Other chemicals produced by damaged cells alert **white blood cells**, the body's main line of defense.

White blood cells are jelly-like blobs that can swim freely through the blood. They can also move easily through inflamed, fluid-filled tissues. Some of the white blood cells make chemical weapons that kill germs or stop them from multiplying. Others swarm over the germs and attack them. But some white blood cells are killed by poisons from the bacteria they have eaten. When this happens, a white sticky substance called **pus** forms. It is made up mainly of the bodies of dead white blood cells, along with the germs they have killed.

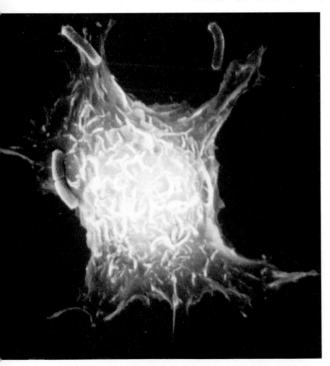

A white blood cell is attacking three bacteria.

Some of your white blood cells make special chemicals called **antibodies**. Your body can make thousands of antibodies, each with a slightly different shape. When a disease germ invades your body, cells of the immune system check out the chemicals (called **antigens**) on its outer surface. Then they look for antibodies that match some of these antigens. As soon as a good match is found, the white blood cells start making more of that particular kind of antibody.

Antibodies attach onto a virus or bacterium, just like the pieces of a jigsaw puzzle fit together. They attach themselves to the germ and stick to it tightly. Antibodies may kill germs, or they may weaken them enough to allow your white blood cells to destroy them.

Did You Know...

It takes about two weeks for the body to produce enough antibodies to fight a new germ.

Once the body has made antibodies against a particular disease germ, it keeps some copies even when the illness is over. Then, if the same kind of germ invades your body again, the immune system can quickly make a new batch of antibodies to fight the invaders before they have a chance to make you sick. That's why you can get chickenpox or measles only once in your life. Doctors say that you are now **immune** to the disease—you can't catch it again. So why can you catch a cold over and over again? That's because there are over 200 different cold viruses; each cold that you get is caused by a different type of germ.

This is the varicella virus that causes chickenpox.

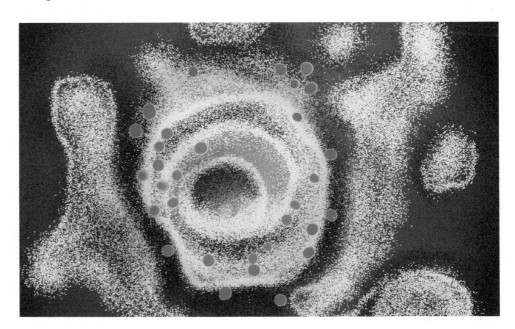

Harmful Germs

Diseases caused by germs are called infectious diseases. You are infected when germs invade your body and start living and multiplying there. Some infectious diseases are **contagious**—passed on from one person to another.

Colds are the most common type of infectious disease, and they are very contagious. Colds are caused by viruses, which can get into your body when you breathe in tiny droplets of moisture from the coughs or sneezes of people around you. Cold viruses may also enter your body if you touch something that somebody with a cold has coughed on, and then rub your nose, mouth, or eyes with your fingers. In the warm, moist lining of the nose and throat, the viruses settle down and start to multiply.

A single cough or sneeze can release hundreds of germs into the air.

Winter Sniffles

Colds occur most often during the winter because people spend more time indoors, making it easier to spread their germs to other people.

Germs, such as bacteria, also live in dirt and dust and can get into your body through a cut or scrape. Some of these bacteria can cause a serious disease called **tetanus**. Stepping on a dirty, rusty nail can push tetanus bacteria deep into your foot. There they can multiply quickly. If tetanus bacteria spread into your bloodstream, their poisons can cause a condition called "lockjaw." Your jaw muscles would get so stiff that you wouldn't be able to move them to eat or talk. Luckily, there are special medicines to protect you from getting very sick if you get dirt into a deep cut.

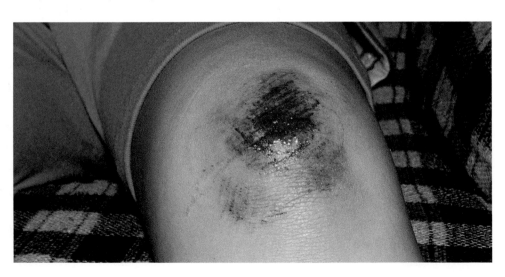

Germs can easily enter the body through an open wound.

Some Common Conditions Caused by Germs

Name of Condition	Kind of Germ	Common Symptoms
Athlete's Foot	Fungus	Red, scaly, itchy rash on feet
Chickenpox	Virus	Fever; headache; red, pimple-like rash
Common Cold	Virus	Sore throat; runny or stuffed-up nose; coughing; sneezing
Ear Infection	Bacterium	Pain and/or swelling in ear; fever
Flu	Virus	Fever; headache; sore throat; coughing; muscle aches and pains
Strep Throat	Bacterium	Fever; sore throat; headache; swollen tonsils; white or yellow patches at back of throat

Swimming in water that contains harmful germs may allow them to get into your body through your nose, mouth, or even ears. Swimmer's ear—a stuffed-up, achy, itchy ear—is caused by bacteria that live in lakes and reservoirs. A child who has had diarrhea and then swims in a pool or reservoir can put millions of bacteria, viruses, and protozoa into the water. These germs can cause stomachaches and diarrhea for everyone who swims in that water. Luckily, swimming pools have chemicals to kill many of these germs.

Germs may also get into your body by hitching a ride on foods you eat and water you drink. If they multiply inside you, they can make you sick. For instance, salmonella is a kind of bacterium that can cause food poisoning. Salmonella has been found mostly in raw and undercooked eggs, poultry, and meat, and in milk products. Symptoms may include fever, headache, diarrhea, nausea, vomiting, and even death in serious cases.

Raw or undercooked meat can cause salmonella.

Cooking and refrigeration may make foods taste better, but they are also ways of protecting us from sickness. Most bacteria that cause food poisoning do not grow in a refrigerator (below 40°F or 4°C), and they are killed by high heat during cooking. Usually food that makes people sick has not been cooked completely—such as a rare hamburger that is still raw inside. Or, the food has been handled by someone with dirty hands and then left out at room temperature.

There are a few kinds of bacteria that are really hard to kill. They can survive even in boiling water by changing into special forms called spores. Bacterial spores are covered by a thick, tough "overcoat" and

Some common mold spores

just rest until conditions are better for growth. The most deadly kind of food poisoning, called botulism, is caused by spore-forming bacteria. These bacteria grow in canned foods that have not been treated properly.

Some infectious diseases spread when a person is bitten by a mosquito or tick that is carrying a disease germ. For instance, a tiny deer tick is a known carrier of a bacterium that causes Lyme disease. A variety of symptoms may develop, including headache, back-ache, nausea, vomiting, chills, swollen lymph glands,

Ticks and insects can carry germs that cause serious diseases.

loss of appetite, sensitivity to light, a stiff neck, and pain and swelling in the joints.

Mosquitoes may carry a disease germ that causes **malaria**. The malaria germ is a protozoan that grows and multiplies inside red blood cells. The tiny germs make the red blood cells burst open. Then they quickly invade new red cells and kill them too. The person suffers from diarrhea, chills, and high fever while the germs are multiplying. Malaria is a very serious disease, but fortunately very rare in the United States and Europe.

The Deadly Three

Just three germs account for more than 5 million deaths in the world each year — half of all the deaths due to infectious diseases. These germs are **HIV**, the TB bacterium, and the malaria protozoan. HIV is a virus that attacks the body's defending white blood cells and causes AIDS. The TB bacterium causes tuberculosis, a serious infection of the lungs. The malaria protozoan causes up to 500 million cases of illness each year and as many as 2 million deaths. Malaria occurs mainly in tropical areas, such as in Africa, Central America, and Southeast Asia.

Do you know why it's so important to brush your teeth every day? Because your mouth is filled with germs. Millions of bacteria come together to feast on the food left in your teeth. As the bacteria grow and multiply, they eventually cover your teeth with a soft, sticky coat of **plaque**. Plaque is a mixture of bits of left-over food, bacteria, and other substances. When you do not clean your teeth regularly, plaque can build up.

When the bacteria grow on the leftover food on your teeth, they make an acid. The acid slowly eats through the tooth's hard outer covering. This may lead to **tooth decay**. Eventually, tooth decay produces a **cavity**, or hole in the tooth.

The acid left from bacteria on your teeth can cause tooth decay.

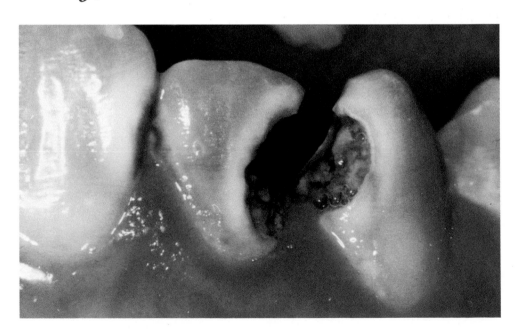

Bacteria can also cause skin problems, such as **acne**. Your skin is covered with tiny hairs. At the base of each hair, there is a tiny gland that pours out **sebum**, an oily substance that keeps your skin soft and smooth. The sebum reaches the surface through tiny **pores** (openings) in the skin. Sometimes oil glands produce so much sebum that it clogs up the oil pores. Bacteria living on the skin can then invade the pores and multiply. Then bacteria, sebum, and dead skin cells are trapped inside the pore.

If the walls of the pore burst open under the surface, sebum, bacteria, and dead skin cells will leak into the skin, causing redness, swelling, and pus—an inflamed sore called a **pimple**. Pimples occur mainly on the face, neck, and back. You should never pick, scratch, or squeeze a pimple. This can spread the bacteria and make the condition much worse.

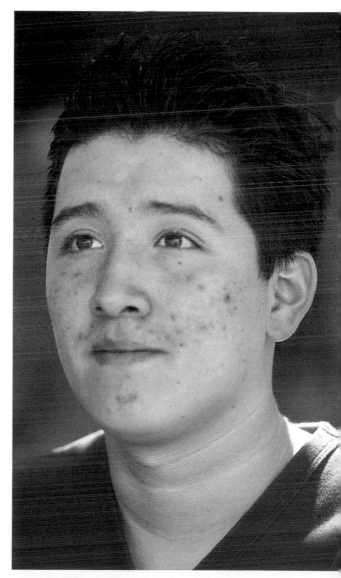

Some bacteria can cause the skin to break out with acne.

Treating Diseases Caused by Germs

Many germ-caused conditions are treated with antibiotics. These are powerful drugs that kill bacteria or stop them from growing. There are many different kinds of antibiotics. Some work best on just a few kinds of bacteria. Others kill many different kinds of harmful germs. Antibiotics fight disease germs in several different ways. For example, an antibiotic may target the part of the bacterium that builds and maintains its **cell wall**. The cell wall is a tough outer covering that protects the bacterium. Damage to it makes the germ helpless against the body's defenses.

30

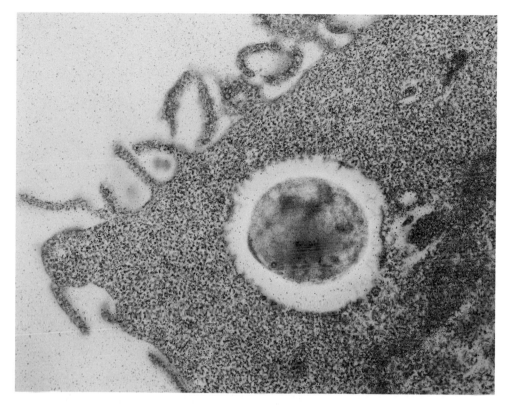

Many antibiotics don't actually kill bacteria but stop them from growing and multiplying. They do this in various ways. Some antibiotics block a bacterium's ability to make proteins. These are important chemicals that are needed to build the cell's structure. Proteins also make special chemicals that run all the cell's activities. There are also antibiotics that keep bacteria from getting energy from their food.

Still other antibiotics target the bacteria's DNA, the chemical that contains the instructions for all the cell's activities and the plans for making new cells. Each time a bacterium divides, it makes a complete copy of its DNA. But when the antibiotic is present, the copies are full of errors. The new bacteria that have this faulty DNA cannot grow and multiply.

The First Antibiotic

Before the 1940s, people did not have an effective weapon against bacteria. Back then, many people died from diseases that can now be successfully treated with antibiotics. The first antibiotic was discovered quite by accident. In 1928, while Alexander Fleming was studying *Staphyloccus* bacteria, he noticed that mold was growing in the culture. Interestingly, there were no bacteria where the mold was. Fleming investigated further and found that there was something in the mold that kept the bacteria from growing. He named this substance "penicillin," since the mold that killed the bacteria was called *Penicillium*.

Penicillin, the first real antibiotic, did not become available for medical use until the 1940s. Since then, antibiotics have saved many lives.

Alexander Fleming

Medical experts worry that people are using antibiotics too much. When bacteria are exposed to an antibiotic, most of them are killed, but some may survive and multiply. These drug-resistant bacteria, which can't be killed by the usual doses of the antibiotic, may be passed on to other people. The more an antibiotic is used, the more likely it is for drug-resistant bacteria to appear and spread. Then even very high doses of the antibiotic will not work against the disease. The bacteria may also become resistant to other drugs.

Antibiotics do not work on colds or other illnesses that are caused by viruses. Antibiotics can treat only infections caused by bacteria. These drugs cannot get into the body cells where viruses hide and multiply.

While no drug can cure a cold, there are certain drugs, called **antivirals**, that are used to treat some viral infections. For example, acyclovir is an antiviral drug that is used to treat chickenpox. Acyclovir works by keeping the viruses from multiplying. When acyclovir is taken within twenty-four hours after the first pox appear, the illness is much milder than usual. The rash goes away much more quickly, and there are fewer sores. But the drug works only if it is given during the first 24 hours of the disease.

Another antiviral drug is AZT. It is often used to treat people with HIV, the virus that causes AIDS. AZT is a chemical that is very similar to one of the building blocks of DNA. Infected cells that are building sets of DNA for HIV viruses may pick up AZT by mistake. But AZT cannot add more building blocks so the DNA chain stops there, and the virus cannot reproduce. However, AZT is not a cure for AIDS and does not stop people from spreading HIV.

The drug AZT is often used to treat HIV patients.

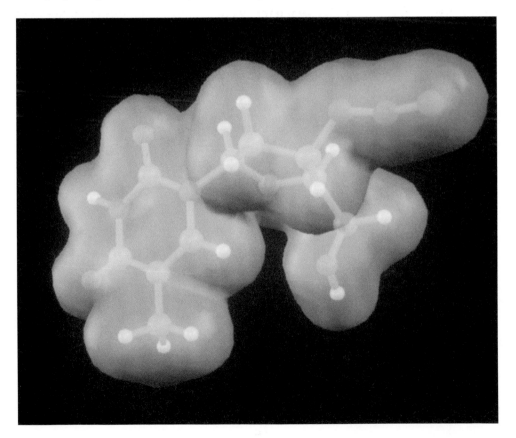

Protect Yourself!

What can you do to avoid germs? Actually, you can't stay away from germs completely—they're everywhere! But there are lots of things you can do to cut down the chances of picking up germs that can make you sick.

First of all, it's very important to keep your shots up to date. At a very young age, you receive various **vaccines**, each of which contains a substance that

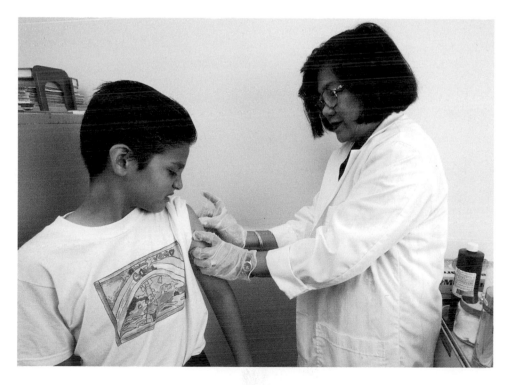

Children get many vaccines to protect them from diseases.

protects you against certain diseases. These diseases include polio, measles, mumps, rubella, diphtheria, pertussis, and tetanus. You may not have heard of some of these diseases. That's because today most people have been vaccinated against these diseases and will not get them even if they are exposed to the germs that cause them.

How Do Vaccines Work?

Vaccines work by fooling the body's defenses. They are made from germs, or parts of them, that have been specially treated so that they cannot make people sick. When a vaccine is injected into your body, your immune system quickly detects the presence of "foreign" chemicals and makes antibodies against them. These antibodies also work against the real germs. So if the disease germs later invade your body, you will be protected against them.

There are also things you can do every day to avoid spreading germs. Most important, wash your hands often, especially before and after meals and after you

Washing your hands often will help protect you from germs.

go to the bathroom. Remember, dirty hands can spread germs from your body wastes to food or to people you touch.

You can protect yourself from many cold viruses by trying not to touch people who have colds. And if you touch things that might carry germs, such as a door knob or the change you get at a store, don't touch your eyes or nose unless you've washed your hands first. If you have a cold, remember to wash your hands often to keep from spreading your viruses to others. It's also a good idea not to share food or drinks with friends. It's not always easy to tell if someone is sick.

Never eat any food that has been sitting out of the refrigerator for a long time. Remember, bacteria grow quickly under these conditions. And if you ever notice fuzzy green or blue mold growing on bread, fruit, or leftovers, don't eat the food. You can't always tell if food is safe just by looking at it. If the food looks funny or smells strange, it's probably not good to eat. But don't taste it to see if it's bad—it could make you sick. Just remember—when in doubt, throw it out!

Activity 2: Grow Your Own Mold

For this activity, you'll need two pie plates, two paper towels, two slices of white bread, plastic wrap, and a magnifying glass. Wet each paper towel and spread one out on each pie plate. Then lay a slice of bread on each paper towel and cover with plastic wrap. Place one pie plate in a closet or some other dark place and the other one in the refrigerator. Leave them alone for three days, then check them each day after that until you see spots on the bread. Which slice of bread gets spots first? Why do you think one slice of bread got spots faster than the other? What color are the spots? Do they look fuzzy or velvety? Look at the spots with a magnifying glass. Depending on the kind of mold, it may look like tiny branching trees, balls on sticks, or some other shape.

Where did the mold come from? Even though the slices of bread looked clean, tiny mold spores, too small to see without a microscope, were floating in the air and settled onto the bread. The wet paper towel provided the moisture they needed to sprout and grow.

Eating healthy foods, exercising regularly, getting enough rest, and washing your hands frequently can also help you to avoid getting sick. Be sure to brush your teeth and keep your clothes, food, and dishes clean. If you can keep yourself healthy and strong, then your body's defenses will be strong enough to fight off invading germs.

Foods for Good Health

Some experts believe that taking vitamin C can help keep your body strong enough to fight off diseases. You can get vitamin C from eating certain fruits and vegetables. They include oranges, grapefruits, lemons, strawberries, broccoli, cauliflower, and tomatoes. Juices, such as orange and grapefruit juice, are good vitamin C foods too. Other vitamins also help to build a strong immune system. These include vitamin A (found in vegetables such as carrots, sweet potatoes, and broccoli) and vitamin E (found in whole grains and also in vegetable oils, margarine, and olives). Minerals, such as selenium and zinc, help too. Meats, fish, eggs, nuts, and whole grains are good sources of these minerals.

Drinking juices with vitamin C can help fight off colds and keep you healthy.

Glossary

acne—a skin condition in which clogged oil pores become infected with bacteria and produce inflamed pimples

antibodies—special germ-fighting chemicals produced by white blood cells

antigens—chemicals on the outer surface of germs that prompt the body to make antibodies

antivirals—drugs that treat certain viral infections

bacterium (plural **bacteria**)—a microscopic single-celled organism; some bacteria can cause illness

cavity—a hole in a tooth, produced by tooth decay

cell wall—the tough, outer covering that protects the bacterium

contagious—easily spread from one person to another

decay bacteria—bacteria that break down animal wastes and the bodies of plants and animals.

disinfectant—something that kills harmful microorganisms.

fungus (plural **fungi**)—an organism that feeds on living or dead matter; includes mushrooms, molds, and yeast

HIV—a virus that attacks white blood cells and causes AIDS

host—a living plant or animal that provides food and shelter for another creature

immune—protected from a disease

immune system—the body's disease-fighting system, which includes white blood cells

inflammation—redness, heat, and swelling that develop when tissues are damaged

Lyme disease—a bacterial disease carried by ticks that may produce a "bull's-eye" rash around a tick bite

malaria—a dangerous disease, often spread by mosquitoes; found mostly in tropical regions

microorganisms—living creatures too small to be seen without a microscope

mucus—a gooey liquid produced by cells in the lining of the nose and breathing passages

pimple—an inflamed sore formed when a clogged oil pore bursts and leaks sebum, bacteria, and dead cell matter, causing inflammation

plaque—a mixture of leftover food, bacteria, and other substances that forms on teeth, especially between teeth and at the edge of the gums

pore—the opening of a skin gland

protozoan (plural **protozoa**)—an animal-like single-celled organism

pus—a whitish substance containing the bodies of dead white blood cells and bacteria

sebum—the oily substance produced by oil glands in the skin

tetanus—a dangerous disease caused by bacteria that can grow only where there is no air, such as inside a deep wound

tooth decay—the effects of acid produced by bacteria in the mouth, which eats through the outer layers of a tooth, producing a hole or cavity

toxins—poisons

vaccine—a substance that stimulates the body's disease-fighting cells to produce antibodies against a particular kind of germ

virus—the smallest kind of germ, which cannot even be seen with an ordinary microscope

white blood cells—jelly-like blood cells that can move through tissues and are an important part of the body's defenses

Learning More

Books

Berger, Melvin. *Germs Make Me Sick*. New York: HarperCollins Publishers, 1995.

Colombo, Luann. *Gross But True Germs*. New York: Simon & Schuster, 1997.

Katz, Bobbi. *Germs! Germs! Germs!* New York: Scholastic Inc., 1996.

Landa, Norbert & Patrick A. Baeuerle. *Your Body's Heroes and Villains: Microexplorers*. Hauppauge, NY: Barron's, 1997.

May, John & Jocelyn Stevenson. *The Magic School Bus: Inside Ralphie, A Book About Germs*. New York: Scholastic Inc., 1995.

Rowan, Kate. *Sam's Science: I Know How to Fight Germs*. Cambridge, MA: Candlewick Press, 1998.

Online Sites
An Ounce of Prevention: Keep the Germs Away
http://www.cdc.gov/ncidod/op/
A Centers for Disease Control site with various links relating to germs and how to protect yourself when you are exposed to them.

Fungus Infections

http://www.quickcare.org/skin/fungus.html

This site has information about various skin conditions caused by fungi, including prevention and treatment.

Germs Make Me Sick

http://www.arthur.k12.il.us/arthurgs/germ.htm

This site provides kid-friendly information about germs and some of the diseases they cause. You can take a quiz to see how much you know about some of the diseases caused by germs.

How Your Immune System Works

http://www.howstuffworks.com/immune_system.htm

This site provides information about the immune system and how it works.

Microbes

http://www.funschool.com/current/games/mic_intro

This site offers interactive games so kids of all ages can have fun learning about germs.

Stalking the Mysterious Microbe!

http://www.microbe.org/

This site follows microbiologist Sam Sleuth in his search to uncover the mysteries of microbes through news stories, experiments, and more.

What Are Germs?

http://kidshealth.org/kid/talk/qa/germs_prt.htm

This site includes easy-to-understand information about germs, kinds of germs, and how you can protect yourself from germs.

Index

Page numbers in *italics* indicate illustrations.

About the Authors

Dr. Alvin Silverstein is a professor of biology at the College of Staten Island of the City University of New York. **Virginia B. Silverstein** is a translator of Russian scientific literature. The Silversteins first worked together on a research project at the University of Pennsylvania. Since then, they have produced six children and more than 180 published books for young people.

Laura Silverstein Nunn, a graduate of Kean College, has been helping with her parents' books since her high school days. She is the coauthor of more than fifty books on diseases and health, science concepts, endangered species, and pets. Laura lives with her husband Matt and their young son Cory in a rural New Jersey town not far from her childhood home.